PRAY WITHOUT CEASING

Pray Without Ceasing

MATTHEW COOPER

TABLE OF CONTENTS

This book is first and foremost dedicated to Jesus, my life changed forever when I let Him into my heart.

Secondly, I want to dedicate this book to my wife Sarah. I'm so grateful to have a supportive and encouraging wife to always be there for me. I love you darling.

Lastly, to my son Will and my future children, I want nothing more for them than to know and love Jesus with all their hearts.

| 1 |

Intro

It's always been on my heart that I would be someone pointing others to Christ. *Ephesians 4:11-13*

11 So Christ himself gave the apostles, the prophets, the evangelists, the pastors and teachers, 12 to equip his people for works of service, so that the body of Christ may be built up 13 until we all reach unity in the faith and in the knowledge of the Son of God and become mature, attaining to the whole measure of the fullness of Christ.

Ephesians 4:11-13 is one of those verses that always stuck out to me and led me to encourage and help others seek His face more than anything else in this world. Through my experiences with the Lord, I've wanted for others to experience Him like I have so that they'd feel the joy, peace and hope that I have had since getting saved. My goal for this book is simple to…practically give helpful resources to develop your prayer life and to stir a hunger and passion to dive deeper into your relationship with Christ.

I don't want this to be some massive read, I want you to be able to dive in and knock it out quickly so that you can apply concepts and begin pressing in for more with Him sooner rather than later. I want to briefly introduce my prayer journey with you all so you know where I've come from and currently where I am with you. I'm not wanting to pretend like I understand everything right away when I got saved or that I haven't gone through challenging times in my prayer life, I just want to be real and honest with you so it can encourage you and challenge you to pursue God more.

My prayer journey has been all over the place from not praying, trying to pray and praying all the time. I got saved right before I went to college. I really didn't have a lot of understanding of many "Christian" things when I got saved. I kind of attended a Presbyterian church with my family growing up so I heard some of the language and stories but that's really all I knew. Once I got to college (Bowling Green State University #TalonsUp) I began seeking Him out probably more than I did my classes. I started to get really involved with Campus Crusade for Christ (Cru) and began learning more and more about who Jesus is and what living as a Christian meant.

Now one of those things that kept coming up was prayer. The only thing I could remember about prayer was praying before meals like I did at Sunday school and at the pre-school I went to. That was probably the extent of what I knew about prayer. My freshman year I was reading the

Bible but my prayer life wasn't existent. It may sound weird but I felt like I didn't know how to pray. After my freshman year I went on a baseball mission trip with Athletes in Action to the Dominican Republic. We played baseball, shared the gospel, helped around communities, it was one of the best experiences of my life. Our leaders would have us pray and I had this fear that they'd call on me to lead the prayer. I had zero desire to pray out loud and especially not in front of people. I made it through the trip only having to pray one time so I made it quick and brief (which isn't bad lol). As I continued to dive into The Bible I kept reading that Jesus would often separate Himself from the disciples and go pray. Then when I read Luke I saw the disciples have a similar question that I had been wondering.

Luke 11:1

Now it came to pass, as He was praying in a certain place, when He ceased, that one of His disciples said to Him, "Lord, teach us to pray, as John also taught his disciples."

I saw that verse and began thinking if the disciples wanted to know how to pray it must be something that I should learn and have a better understanding of. I started going to a mid-week service in Toledo near my college and I saw people there pray with authority, power, passion and joy. I saw them sit and lay face down desperately praying. As I hung around them and listened while they shared verses with me I started to get a better grasp of prayer and what it looked like and meant. That taste of prayer and spending time with the Father hit me and all I wanted was that intimacy with the Lord and to pray for people. Once I graduated I moved to Kalamazoo, Michigan and I met someone at a young adult night at a church I was checking out and he told me about a house of prayer in the city (Kalamazoo House of Prayer). I knew of IHOP (not the pancake one lol) and was familiar with how it flowed and the reliance on prayer that they taught but never really experienced it before. I started going to KHOP a lot and eventually started leading prayer sets there and that's when I discovered the beauty of prayer and the importance of how prayer leads to deeper fellowship and relationship with the Father.

A few years went by and I found my stunning, beautiful and amazing wife. I moved to Erie, PA to start our life together. Once we got married we would put worship music on and just sit with Him to be in His presence , it's one of my favorite things to do with her since we are both super hungry for

Him. Soon enough a little revivalist came into our lives. Now it has been quite a transition and still is for the both of us who are used to spending long times with Him but now we have our son crawling around and taking all our attention. Our time with the Lord now looks completely different and it can be frustrating when we don't get the time we used to have with Him and to just be able to sit there for however long we wanted. So our prayer lives have had to adjust to nap schedules, any free time we have, or just while we are spending time with our son. Luckily, we are helping lead our churches weekly worship/intercession set that creates time for us to press in and have our son be in the environment to experience His presence.

So I hope that my story shows that it is a journey. We all are in different seasons with the

Lord and at times we may have a very fruitful time with Him interceding and praying. And other times it can be challenging and difficult to have time to connect with Him. Like I stated at the beginning of this intro, my goal is for this book to encourage, build hunger and give practical resources to develop your prayer life into a deeper place than ever before so I hope that it does exactly that!

| 2 |

The Importance of Prayer

So why should we pray? It's something I touched on briefly in the intro, if one of the main questions that the disciples had for Jesus was about prayer there must be some significant value for it. The disciples spent three years with Jesus and saw every miracle and every deliverance; yet never asked Him to teach them how to be a better preacher, it was how to teach them to pray. Pastor Andrew Murray, a missionary to South Africa in the 1800s said this about Jesus teaching on prayer,

"Jesus never taught His disciples how to preach, only how to pray. He did not speak much of what was needed to preach well, but much of praying well. To know how to speak to God is more than knowing how to speak to man. Not power with men, but power with God is the first thing." That statement right before the last sentence I think summarizes it beautifully in saying that "knowing how to speak to God is more than knowing how to speak to man". As believers we are always trying to gain a deeper understanding and connection with God, so we better be able to communicate and foster that relationship. On top of that we are called to "Be anxious for nothing, but in everything by prayer and supplication, with thanksgiving, let your requests be made known to God" (Philippians 4:5-7). Take all our issues, concerns, pains, fears, doubts, EVERY-

THING to Him. In any relationship if it lacks communication it will be rocky, difficult to maintain and will lack trust and faith.

Luke 11:1

"Now it came to pass, as He was praying in a certain place, when He ceased, that one of His disciples said to Him, "Lord, teach us to pray, as John also taught his disciples."

In Luke 11:1 the first sentence says that Jesus was praying but then right after that it says once he stopped the disciples asked about how to pray. I think the disciples were so captivated by how Jesus prayed that they wanted to take their prayer to a deeper place. They could tell Jesus' closeness to the Father through seeing Him pray. I went through the Gospels and found 38 separate times where Jesus would pray. It's something that is littered throughout the Bible. (Luke 3:21-22) (Mark

1:35-36)(Luke 5:16)(Luke 6:12-13)(Matt 11:25-26)(John 6:11)(Matt 14:19) (Mark 6:41((Luke 9:16)(Matt 14:23) (Mark 6:46) (John 6:15)(Mark 7:31-37)(Matt 15:36)(Mark 8:6-7)(Luke 9:18)(Luke 9:28-29)(Luke 10:21)(Luke 11:1)(John 11:41-42)(Matt 19:13-15)(Mark 10:13-16)(Luke 18:15-17) (John 12:27-28)(Matt 26:26)(Mark 14:22-23)(Luke 22:19)(Luke 22:31-32)(John 17:1-26)(Matt 26:36-46)(Luke 22:39-46)(Mark 14:32-42) (Luke 23:34)(Matt 27:46) (Mark 15:34)(Luke 23:46)(Luke 24:30)(Luke 24:50-53). As a son I think we always have a desire inside of us to do what our father does and for him to be proud of us. Growing up I can remember always wanting to be around my dad and help however I could with what project he was doing. I wanted to be like him and do what he did. Even now in my own life I see my son crawling around, following me in our house. He's always so fascinated with what I'm doing. The desire in his little heart to see what his dad is doing. He is looking up to me for everything, I mean my wife and I are the ones who's lives he's going to be impacted by the most in his developmental years. On a side note that's why it's so important for parents to be conscious of what we are doing and saying around our little ones (I know I have to check myself sometimes). Jesus would continue to draw near to the Father time and time again to come to Him. Jesus didn't stop coming to the Father even when He was nailed to the cross Jesus called out to God (Mt: 27:46-47). Jesus would always make time for the Father, this is a point I want to come back to in the next chapter to help our own prayer lives to go to another place.

Relationship with the Father is essential in living life as a Christian. Communication with Him is a necessity in maintaining our connection with Him. In the Bible it talks about coming to Him and drawing near to the Father.

James 4:8

Draw near to God and He will draw near to you.

Cleanse your hands, you sinners; and purify your hearts, you

double-minded.

Building intimacy, storing oil with the Father draws our hearts closer to Him. The time we spend with Him not only in communication but just being in His presence is going to transform our minds and lives into more of the image of Christ. I can remember hearing so much from my early years of being saved, constantly being told the importance of "quiet time" and spending time with the Lord. It took some time to understand what it looked like for me to read, pray and press in with Him. Since I really didn't know what to do since I was new in my faith I tried to make it as simple as I could. I read a few verses and just prayed some typical prayers for people. Although this was good for me to start with I felt that there was a deeper level I wanted to go with Him than where I was at. One of the most important things that helped me grow deeper in intimacy with the Father was simply sitting with Him.

My friends and I would gather every Monday night to worship/pray and just be with Him. This time really helped shape my desire to go deeper with the Lord and simply spend time with Him. From that time I would ask questions, soak, meditate and learn ways to enter in to grow my intimacy. In *Matthew 6:19-21* Jesus is preaching the Sermon on the Mount and He talks about laying up treasures in Heaven. There are many ways you can break down these verses but when I think of verse 20 specifically about laying up treasures in Heaven I think of what am I being consumed with? Is it time? Possessions? Something else? Am I building a foundational relationship with Jesus here on Earth and storing my oil or am I getting consumed by Netflix, YouTube, Social Media, etc. I'm the first to admit I get lost on YouTube rabbit holes and waste time that I could be using more wisely. I once heard during a Bible Study someone say this of Mary of Bethany and the oil she anointed Jesus with. They posed this question which to this day burns within me, what if her oil was the time she spent with Him? It's said that the oil Mary anointed Jesus with was super expensive and valuable. That oil she poured on Him was said to be still lingering while Jesus hung on the cross. What if the time she spent adoring Him and at His feet caused the oil to be so fragrant? Once I heard this I began to think well...is the oil I'm storing that fragrant? Would it last for days? Does it smell weird? Mary of Bethany has become one of my favorite characters of the Bible and it's simply due to her actions of coming to His feet again and again. She doesn't say much but her actions speak WAY louder than her words. When the other disciples questioned Mary's choice Jesus said in Matthew 26, "what this woman has done will also be told as a memorial to her." She will be remembered for this act of being at Jesus' feet and anointing Him for burial.

Just as Jesus would go away to be with the Father it's important we follow that same example and make time in our days to be in His presence. Even if it's only for a short amount of time we are at least being obedient and doing what He has written. To enter into a deeper place of prayer we must establish our relationship with Him and build intimacy. If we aren't aware of who He is, then how can we pray to Him?

That intimacy and time with Him will only stir more hunger for Him and isn't that a part of our desires as Christians, to be close to Him and know Him more? Jesus hits on this in the Sermon on the Mount,

Matthew 5:6

Blessed are those who hunger and thirst for righteousness, For they shall be filled.

He clearly states that those who hunger and thirst for righteousness will be filled. At the time of this message being preached the very ones listen-

ing did know what it really meant to be hungry and

thirsty. Compare that to today in the West where

we have such access to food and drink. Do we re-

ally know what it means to be hungry and thirsty? I

mean I once went a whole month without ice cream

and I thought that was super difficult. This conver-

sation could easily lead into one about fasting but

that would probably be another chapter or book

even. Briefly, fasting combined with prayer and a

correct heart posture can lead to fresh hunger for

God. Fasting is an incredible gift that we can use to

draw nearer to the Father. I found this excerpt from

a sermon by John G. Lake that discusses hunger.

"Hunger is a mighty good thing. It is the greatest per-

suader I know of. It is a marvelous mover. Nations have

learned that you can do most anything with a populace until they get hungry. But when they get hungry you want to watch out. There is a certain spirit of desperation that accompanies hunger.

The stories you hear of the underground church in China where they kiss their Bibles when they receive them. Stories of the boldness of missionaries around the world and especially in the 10/40 Window. A real quick note if you are unfamiliar with the 10/40 Window it is an area of North Africa, the Middle East and Asia approximately between 10 degrees north and 40 degrees north latitude, which contains the largest unreached people groups who haven't heard of the Gospel. Hungry people will do anything for the Lord! When we spend that time and create history with Him that fans the flame of our hunger for Him. When we pray and see breakthrough, when we pray and see a miracle, when we pray and see XYZ our faith increases, our love increases, and our hunger increases!

Lastly, in this chapter I wanted to touch on why people don't pray and the fears that we can sometimes believe or come into agreement with. I was reading the book *Praying Like Monks Living Like Fools by Tyler Staton* (highly recommend this book!) and early on in the book he addresses the fears of why people don't pray and the excuses people have. From all the books and resources I've read about prayer I've never come across anything that mentioned the fears some have about prayer. It really stuck out to me because I realized I definitely had fears when it came to my own prayer journey. I want to pray right now to rebuke and come against any lies, misconception, fears and doubts that you may have with prayer!

Father, I pray right now that you would refresh and renew my mind with how I view prayer. Let your truths of who you are overcome me and lead me in my prayer time with you. I reject any lies I once believed about prayer and come against any fears that I may have. I want to draw near to you and stand in the gap for ones who need you. I love you Father in Jesus name I pray! Amen.

The biggest fear I had when I first was saved and started to pray was the fear of not having the "right" words. I feared that my prayers didn't sound "good enough" or weren't spiritual enough or long enough. Not only when I'd be praying alone but even more so when I prayed out loud in front of people. I truly was afraid to pray and tried everything I could to avoid praying in public. I felt like I had to have the best sounding and most spiritual prayer or whatever it was and all of that is not true at all! Jesus' prayers were simple and most of them weren't crazy long. When Jesus prayed for the sick he'd simply pray," Get up, pick up your mat and walk." (John 5:8) and "Come out of the man, you evil spirit." (Mark 5:8). And if we aren't sure what to pray, the Holy Spirit will give you words (Luke 12:12) all you have to do is open your mouth!

Another fear that I read from *Praying Like Monks* which surprised me was the fear of silence. I was kind of expecting fear of silence in terms of not hearing the audible voice of God or getting some exact statement from God. Many people struggle with waiting on the Lord and hearing from Him. The fear in the book was more so talking about waiting on the Lord in silence and silence in general. As a society we need entertainment, noise, whatever it is so that it isn't quiet. I know I get caught up some-times when I should turn the music off and just be still with Him but you know I love that song and it gets me in the right mood. Dallas Willard said of si-lence, "Silence is frightening because it strips us as nothing else does, throwing us upon the stark re-alities of our life." It's easy for us to talk about Je-sus, sing the songs, listen to the sermon, ext. But when it comes down to it can we just sit like Mary and be still? I'm sure Paul wasn't jamming to the latest UPPERROOM album while he was in prison, he had his thoughts and his time talking and com-muning with the Lord. Yes, I love worship music and soaking and all that jazz but sometimes let's take a step back and be still with Him in silence and just listen. Many may fear the awkwardness of silence or feel like it's boring. If we are engaging in silence it's not going to be awkward and it's not going to be boring. I can remember a time I was leading a prayer set in Kalamazoo and the Lord stopped the meeting and transformed it into a beautiful peaceful quiet moment with Him. The worship leader just stopped and raised her arms and sat in awe of who He is. I had this feeling of repentance sweep over me and I went to the ground repenting and thanking Him for what He delivered me from and the ways He transformed my life. It was a beautiful moment I cherish to this day. Silence shouldn't be feared but welcomed. Personally, I know I need to have that on my mind more often than I do because when I've surrendered my preferences and let Him come He's always shown up. Sometimes we overthink prayer to a point where we become scared and fearful. We should be confident in knowing He is listening to our prayers and is forever making intercession for us! In the next chapter we will go more in-depth with this thought.

Revelation 5:8

"Now when He had taken the scroll, the four living creatures and the twenty-four elders fell down before the Lamb, each having a harp, and golden bowls full of incense, which are the prayers of the saints."

I hope that this chapter has been an encouragement to some of the reasons why we should pray and why it's critical for our relationship with Jesus. I wanted to end with a quote that I recently heard this year from Pastor Lyle Phillips of Legacy Church in Nashville, TN and I think it's one of my favorites!

"Big intimacy, big impact, history belongs to the prayer warriors!"

| 3 |

Jump Start Your Prayer Life

Of the chapters in this book I believe this is the most important one. I want to help give practical, easy to learn and understand tips and ways to engage with the Lord via prayer. For the first few years of being a Christian I never really had practical tips to help me engage with the Lord in prayer. The most common response I'd hear is just sit and talk with Him. Which is a solid response but in my mind I would think, well what do I say? How do I start? Are there specific things I need to pray? How long should I pray? How can I go deeper? Things like those thoughts would come into my mind. As my journey with the Father continued I feel like I was able to flow with Him in those prayer times and was able to answer those questions. But I also had some great advice and mentors who helped me with answering some of those questions and giving tips to make that time easier to engage with Him.

The first thing I want to discuss before we go any further is understanding who we are praying to. If we are communicating and praying to God shouldn't we know who He is? It would be hard to pray for healing if we don't believe God can heal. Knowing the Fathers heart I believe helps us enter into prayer and go to places we might not have gone before with Him. When we have faith in knowing who He is, that will fuel our prayer life and encourage us to have confidence in what we are praying.

There are a few verses I wanted to go through that go into this idea of understanding who God is when we enter into prayer.

Matthew 16:13-20

"When Jesus came into the region of Caesarea Philippi, He asked His disciples, saying, "Who do men say that I, the Son of Man, am?" So they said, "Some say John the Baptist, some Elijah, and others Jeremiah or one of the prophets." He said to them, "But who do you say that I am?" Simon Peter answered and said, "You are the Christ, the Son of the living God." Jesus answered and said to him, "Blessed are you, Simon Bar-Jonah, for flesh and blood has not revealed this to you, but My Father who is in heaven. And I also say to you that you are Peter, and on this rock I will build My church, and the gates of Hades shall not prevail against it. And I will give you the

keys of the kingdom of heaven, and whatever you bind on earth will be bound in heaven, and whatever you loose on earth will be loosed in heaven." Then He commanded His disciples that they should tell no one that He was Jesus the Christ."

In verse 13 Jesus is coming to His disciples and asking *"Who do men say that I am"*. So they begin to tell Him all the different people and thoughts that people have about who Jesus is. In which all of the responses underestimate who Jesus really is, sure they give Him honor and re-spect but none of them accurately depict who He truly is. Then Jesus followed that up with a question to the dis-ciples about who they thought He was. Peter speaks up and pretty such says that he understands not only is Je-sus God's only Messiah but He also is God himself. Peter was able to come to the conclusion that Jesus was exactly who He said He was and truly was the Messiah. Peter hung with Jesus day in day out, saw the miracles, heard his sermons and saw how Jesus lived. He was confident in knowing that from all that he witnessed he was truly following the Lord of Lords and King of Kings. Like stated before, sometimes I feel when we pray we don't always pray from that place of confidence in knowing who we are talking to. What if we prayed with the expectation to see healing? To see Him provide? To see him restore that relationship? When we come to the revelation that Peter had, our prayers are going to be way more confident because we believe who Jesus really is. We then will more easily be able to pray for those things because we really know He is healer, provider, restorer, Prince of Peace, ext. Our confidence will increase a bunch, which leads into the next verse that I thought is helpful in talking about this topic.

1 John 5:14-15

"Now this is the confidence that we have in Him, that if we ask anything according to His will, He hears us. And if we know that He hears us, whatever we ask, we know that we have the petitions that we have asked of Him."

When we are praying we better believe that God hears us. This verse states exactly that. How can we pray in confidence if we don't even believe God will answer our prayer? Sounds like a difficult thing to do if you don't believe that He would answer what is on your heart. It's important for us to know that we have His ear! He is listening to every single prayer that we are releasing into the atmosphere. They aren't just going up and floating away, they are actually going up into the throne room and filling the golden bowls with incense. We need to position our hearts when we pray to this level of confidence. When Mary approaches Jesus in John 11 she says ,*"Lord, if you had been here, my brother would not have died."* Both Mary

and her sister Martha said the same thing to Jesus, but I

think Mary had more confidence for who Jesus was. The

Bible says in the next verse that Jesus was moved by her

tears which led Him to ask where Lazarus was so that he

could raise him from the dead. Mary is one of my favorite

characters in the Bible outside of Jesus and this small act I

believe is something to note. She's coming from this place

of expectation that if Jesus was really there the other day

then Lazarus wouldn't have died. She fully expected Jesus

to heal him and had no doubts at all. She had confidence

in this dire situation that her brother would be healed and

knew Jesus was Messiah and that He was Healer. I think

if we were in this moment with Jesus and the sisters we

would be able to tell the difference in the heart posture of

both Mary and Martha. They said the same thing but Je-

sus was moved by Mary and not Martha. Not only when

we pray should we be confident in knowing that we have His ear but also praying from a place of victory! I think that goes along with having confidence in our prayers but knowing that we have the victory and praying from that place of being an overcomer, dead to sin alive in Him and that the enemy has no hold on us. Before I go any further it's important to note here that just because we are praying with confidence it doesn't mean God will answer our prayer right away. Again, it's His timing not ours. If we are living and praying from that place our prayers are going to be bolder and sound a lot different than ones who are praying from a place of uncertainty. A practical step in wanting more confidence and better understanding of who God is would be 1. Going into the Bible and finding as many scriptures as you can about this and 2. Simply asking God to give you more confidence and ask Holy Spirit for more revelation of who God is.

Like I stated at the beginning of this chapter I want to make this super practical and easy to understand. One of the easiest tips that I can give you is to set a time and place and show up. Setting up a time and place helps create intimacy with the Lord, after all, prayer is a relationship. For the first five months of my relationship with my wife we were six hours apart and had to FaceTime, text and do all the mobile things to communicate with one another. We had to make that effort to say hey I really want to continue getting to know you and take our relationship to deeper places. It would have been easy for both of us to put it on the back burner since we weren't near each other. Since we both had a desire to see where this relationship would go we made the effort to make time for FaceTime calls, traveling to see each other and things like that. I know certain seasons of life are different and setting a time and place might be easier during some seasons of life and others it's more difficult.

Like I mentioned in the intro, since becoming a father my setting a place and time with the Lord looks completely different than it once did. I think the key I've been realizing is that if I show up for even a minute He honors that and will still meet me. When I was in college I had a little corner in our second floor house where I wrote prayer requests and every morning I'd spend 20 minutes before my classes and I'd sit with the Lord and build that intimacy with Him while I also interceded for those on the list I had. For a while I was a part of a ministry called The Morivan Watch where we'd zoom call every Tuesday morning from 5:00am -6:00am and press in and pray the whole time. This was helpful for me to have a place to pray and connect with the Lord. If you're interested in hearing more about The Morivan Watch I'd highly suggest you check out their website mwatch.org. Another practical tip is downloading The Inner Room app on your phone. I've recently discovered this tool and it has been really beneficial to me. It sends you a notification on your phone to take time to pray. I set mine to 7:00 am and every morning I'll get that notification and I'll take a couple of minutes and thank the Lord and pray whatever is on my heart at the moment. It can be a tough discipline to get into but it is one that is vital in our walks with the Lord. When we look at Jesus' life He often withdrew and prayed. Jesus would set a time and place and would commune with the Father. Whatever it looks like for you, set a time and come for Him. If it's one hour or one minute make the commitment to the Lord to create deeper levels of intimacy in your relationship with Him.

One of the more revelatory ideas that I heard, which has transformed my prayer life is to not come in with your list at first. Yes, you heard me right. I feel at times when people think of prayer they think of so and so telling them to pray for their relative that is having surgery or petitioning before the Lord with help on a decision. Yes, we need to pray for those things but a verse that has challenged me to not immediately come in with these requests and petitions is Psalm 100:4.

> *Enter into His gates with thanksgiving, And into His courts with praise. Be thankful to Him, and bless His name.*

How does it say to enter into His gates? With thanksgiving, not with my demands and my list. Prayer starts with God not with us. Come with our offering of praise and thanksgiving first! Once we've given Him this offering then let's ask to heal our relative and give us discernment in this situation. God deserves all the praise, honor and glory, if we want to get to that deeper place with Him then we must start with thanksgiving. Even for worship sets, I'm not a musician or worship leader but again if we are entering with thanksgiving, then according to scriptures we are going to be welcomed into His gates. I believe that if worship is started from a song/heart posture of thanksgiving that set will be able to get to a deeper level with the Lord than one that does not begin with thanksgiving. Got a little sidetracked with how thanksgiving can/should be incorporated in a worship setting but back to prayer. To give some more scripture let's look at a couple prayers that Jesus prayed during His life on Earth.

At the beginning of this chapter we talked a bit about having confidence in who we are praying to and from that place we should have confidence as well in our prayer.

Matthew 11:25

I thank You, Father, Lord of heaven and earth, that You have hidden these things from the wise and prudent and have revealed them to babes.

John 11:41-42

And Jesus lifted up His eyes and said, "Father, I thank You that You have heard Me. And I know that You always hear Me, but because of the people who are standing by I said this, that they may believe that You sent Me.

Matthew 6:9

Our Father in Heaven, hallowed be Your name.

Both times in the verses from John and Matthew Jesus starts with offering thanks to the Father. Then Jesus goes into why He is thanking God for the answered prayer. Now the last text is the beginning of the Lord's Prayer. Hallowed by definition means holy, sacred. It's not exactly thanksgiving but it is praise and giving adoration and ac-knowledgment to who the Father is. To wrap up this point again, come in for Him first then bring your requests. Prayer is a relationship.

Along with having confidence in knowing who we are praying to, the idea of praying from the place of victory I think goes hand in hand with that confidence. When we are praying with the heart posture of victory knowing the price that was paid on the cross and what Jesus endured for us it's hard to not trust Him and lay it all out there. Like I mentioned at the beginning of the chapter, how can we pray to God if we don't believe who He is? How can we pray to God if we don't believe He rose on the third day? If we don't believe in the victory that took place on the cross how can we be confident in our prayers? At times I think as Believers we lose sight of the cross and forget the power and significance it has on our faith. We need a deeper revelation of the cross! I think when we are able to grasp even a bit more of the significance of the cross our prayers will transform from just a "wish" to a confident request that is from a heart posture of victory and expectancy. We need to pray from this place of VICTORY! We don't need to worry about fighting against the enemy or be burdened with whatever is on our heart. When we are in victory and confidence we can easily lift our burdens to the Lord knowing He is listening.

1 Corinthians 15:57

But thanks be to God! He gives us the victory through our

Lord Jesus Christ.

To remind myself of this, a helpful tip I picked up is literally imagining myself in the throne room before God. Picturing all of Revelation 4, the four living creatures, the emerald rainbow, 24 elders clothed in white, the seven lamps of fire and the sea of glass. For me, something about putting myself in the throne room made it become more real and just easier to put my heart in the right posture to pray. If I'm having trouble remembering I have His ear, then practically imagining myself before the throne helped me. If I'm having difficulty not trusting who God is, picturing myself in the throne room helps me remember all the miracles, all the testimonies and the majesty of God which brings back my trust and confidence in who I'm praying to. Hopefully that makes sense, I believe small things like that can help make prayer feel more like a con-

versation between best friends than some random awk-

ward conversation about requests I may have. I've said it

before and I'll say it again, prayer is a relationship. The

more comfortable we feel talking to God the easier prayer

will feel. It's a muscle that needs to be worked out. When

I first became a Christian it took me a while before I re-

ally started to pray and once I did it became so easy and

natural to press in, pray with confidence and pray from the

place of victory.

Next, I want to talk about apostolic prayers. Apos-

tolic prayers are simply prayers that are written in the Word

of God and were spoken by Jesus and the apostles. Apos-

tolic prayers are great really in any situation but I feel that

they are super useful if you are stuck and aren't sure what

to pray. Since they are written by the finger of God there

should be no fear in saying the wrong thing during prayer (which there shouldn't be anyway, I pray against the fear of praying for anyone struggling with that in Jesus name!).

I want to go over a couple of reasons why apostolic prayers are important and why we should incorporate them more in our prayer times. For starters they are Holy Spirit inspired. Apostolic prayers are the ones that burn in the heart of God enough for Him to put them in the Bible forever. The Holy Spirit put these prayers in the mouths of the apostles, and they give us a glimpse of what God desires to do in and through His people. If the apostles prayed these prayers they must be good enough for us to pray as well! Sometimes when we don't know what to pray we just need to ask the Holy Spirit to help us and since these prayers have been inspired by the Holy Spirit it seems like it's a pretty solid word from

Him to pray. Another reason why they are important is because they are God-centered prayers. We can learn a lot more about God when we are focused on praying to Him than when we are rebuking the enemy. God's model of prayer is desired to be centered around Him not around the enemy or ourselves.

Next, apostolic prayers are positive and not negative. It says in *Philippians 9:1* "*And this I pray, that your love may abound still more and more in knowledge and all discernment.*" Instead of praying for hatred to be removed from a situation that might be difficult. We should be praying positively, that guards us against growing frustrated and angry. Instead we get to grow in love for the people we're praying for. When I first was saved I'd hear our leaders in the campus ministry I was a part of talk about the upside down Kingdom. This idea goes along with that. Things in the Kingdom of Heaven don't go with how things on this Earth go. *Matthew 20:16* is a great example of this, *"So the last will be first, and the first last. For many are called, but few chosen."* For example Paul wrote in *Philippians 1:21, "to live is Christ and to die is gain."* Not really a statement you'd hear from many in our society. Dying typically isn't looked at as a positive or gain. Even praying for our enemies, like what? Especially something that is positive and not trying to make things worse for them. Having these prayers at your disposal can make those tough prayers a bit easier and give language to what you may be feeling in that situation. Blessing people always feels better than receiving. Lastly, apostolic prayers are super flexible. By that I mean if you look hard enough in the Bible you'll find ones for a ton of different situations.

Here is a very very short list of apostolic prayers that can be used.

- For wisdom and revelation in the knowledge of God (Eph. 1:17)
- For strengthening with might in the inner being (Eph. 3:16, Col. 1:11)
- For love to abound (Phil. 1:9, 1 Thes. 3:12)
- For the knowledge of God's will (Col. 1:9)
- That the Word of the Lord would rapidly spread (2 Thes. 3:1)
- To glorify God in unity, with joy, peace, and hope (Rom. 15:5-6, 13)
- To preach with boldness and power (Acts 4:29-30)

Just a helpful tip that can guide you a bit more, if you search for apostolic prayers on any search engine you'll find a lot bigger lists that can be way more detailed. But keep an eye open when you are reading the Bible and you'll probably catch them.

One of the most helpful tips that I have learned is called "Pray-Reading". It's exactly what you think it is when you read that name. While you are going through scripture you turn that verse or passage into a prayer. It is not enough just to study the Word we are meant to talk with God as we read it. Studying the Bible is meant to create an active dialogue in our hearts with God. One way in which we gain strength in our prayer lives is by feeding on the Word through engaging in conversation with God as we read it. When you pray the Word, you and the Spirit flow together, resulting in Him teaching you in a way that is tailor-made for your life. When you talk to God while reading the Word, you say new things to God.

1 John 2:27

"But the anointing which you have received from Him abides in you, and you do not need that anyone teach you; but as the same anointing teaches you concerning all things, and is true, and is not a lie, and just as it has taught you, you will abide in Him."

This verse I believe connects well with the idea of how prayer reading can be a tool to let the Holy Spirit speak to us through reading and praying scripture. John's message is simple. Because of the anointing of the Holy Spirit given to all believers, they possess the resources for knowing the truth.

There are a few techniques that I've learned that I want to share that I believe are super beneficial when connecting with the Lord via prayer reading. The first breaks it down really easily to understand when you're reading the Word. The best way to explain these is giving examples so I hope that as I give these examples that it makes sense to you. Let's say that you are reading through John 15. You come to verse 12 which says, *"My command is this: Love each other as I have loved you."* This verse really begins to hit you and minister to you. Now we can turn this verse into prayer. We can ask the Father to help us love those who are difficult, have a soft heart for those in our sphere of influence, or let us receive His love so that we can love others. I hope that makes sense, whatever in the scripture you are reading that is ministering to you, let His words from those scriptures and what is going on in your heart become a prayer.

Besides the simple technique that I just shared, there are two concepts that we can look for in the Word as we read and let that translate into prayer. These concepts to look for are promises to believe and exhortations to obey. When we are going through the Word and we see either one of those types of ideas in scripture it is an opportune moment to pray into those ideas. When we come across a *promise to believe* while reading the Word, we turn it into conversation with Jesus. There are many verses with promises to believe, such as "God loves His people" and "God forgives us" and "God will provide for and guide us." Or even promises in terms of covenants. I encourage you to do two things when talking to God about a *promise to believe*. First, thank God for that truth; second, ask the Spirit to give you more understanding of it. First, we thank God for a particular truth and turn it into a declaration of thanksgiving or trust. For example, when reading that Jesus loves you as the Father loves Him, pray, "Thank You, Jesus, that You love me with the same intensity with which the Father loves You." *As the Father loved Me, I also have loved you; abide in My love." (John 15:9).* Second, we ask God for more understanding of a specific truth. For example, while reading that Jesus loves you as the Father loves Him, pray, "Jesus, give me more understanding about how You love me with the same intensity with which the Father loves You."

Now when we read *exhortations* (an address or communication emphatically urging someone to do something) *to obey* in the Word, we can turn them into conversation with Jesus, just as we do with God's promises. Many verses *exhort us to obey* related to our time, money, speech, work, attitudes, food, drink, eyes, sexuality, service, relationships, etc. Jesus exhorted His people to abide in His love. Obeying Him involves dwelling on, or focusing on, His love searching it out and going deeper to understanding it. So we could again use John 15:9 to not only pray from a place of promise but also an exhortation. I will encourage you again to do two things I do when talking to God about an *exhortation to obey.* First, I commit myself to obey that truth; second, I ask the Holy Spirit to help me. First, we commit to obey a truth, we make simple declarations of our resolve to obey it. In this case we pray, "Jesus, I commit to abide in and focus on Your love. I set my heart to study and search out this truth from Your Word and to live in it." Second, we ask God to empower us to obey the particular truth. We ask Him to help us by giving us wisdom, motivation, and power to obey in specific areas. For example, when reading that we are to abide in love, simply pray, "Jesus, help me to abide in Your love."

I hope that those explanations are clear and make sense in how to use God's words from His holy scripture and turn them into powerful prayers. An encouragement would be, don't overthink it! It really is that simple, noticing scriptures we are reading that are sticking out to us and when our hearts get burdened or moved by them using them as a place to pray. Like I stated with apostolic prayers, we are praying His word so its going to be good since we are basing our prayers on His word and truths.

Lastly, I want to talk about an acronym that was introduced to me by a mentor when I was in college. This acronym is for when you may be stuck and not sure what to pray, having a hard time entering into prayer or just need something you can do to start the dialogue with the Lord. I've found that it is extremely useful and practical in helping develop a deeper prayer life. The acronym is FELLOWSHIP. Super easy to remember right? A vital part of life as a Christian is fellowshiping with fellow believers. When we begin thinking about the importance of fellowship, hopefully now the concepts of this acronym will begin to come to our mind and stick easier since the word is one that is spoken a lot in Christian circles. I'll quickly lay them out for you and then go into a little more depth with them and give brief examples of a prayer for each.

Fear of God

Endurance

Love

Light of Glory

One Thing

Worthy

Speech

Humility

Insight

Peace and Joy

To kick it off is F which is fear of God. The verse that always strikes me when I think of the fear of the Lord is Proverbs 9:10 *"The fear of the LORD is the beginning of wisdom, And the knowledge of the Holy One is understanding."* Having a proper fear of the Lord is the BEGINNING of wisdom. I feel that we often want to seek wisdom and knowledge a lot when we pray for certain things. And according to Proverbs if we are in the fear of the Lord we step into both of those. The word fear itself is translated in Hebrew to the word *Yirah,* which means having a sense of awe, wonder, amazement, mystery and adoration. In my opinion the Church needs to talk more about the fear of the Lord and dispel any lies and misconceptions that can arise with it. It's a beautiful thing and I think it needs to be communicated more so that we can have a better understanding and be more in awe of the Father. If you don't know the exact words of how to pray for this here is a little help. *Release the spirit of the fear of God in my heart. It is far easier to resist compromise when we feel even a small measure of the fear, or awe, of God in our hearts. Ask Him to cause you to delight in the fear of the Lord (Isa. 11:3) and to strike your heart with the majesty and awesome dread of God (Isa. 8:13).*

Endurance- As believers I feel that we all long to hear "*Well done good and faithful servant.*" We want to know that we ran the race well, and that we spent our days doing the will of the Father. The Bible makes it clear that this is easier said than done. We need to run the marathon and not the 100m race. Endurance is crucial for our lives following Christ. I'm a revival history buff. I love reading stories of revival and all the details of how and why they began and the outcomes of them. One of the most significant details about the Hebrides Revival (1949-1953) is that it is documented that there was very little to any backsliding by Christians who were saved during this movement. I was very involved in campus ministry during my college years and one of the saddest things I've seen as I've gotten older is seeing friends I did ministry with walk away from their faith. The excitement of getting born again is amazing, but we can't get burnt out by a quick burst. We need consistency and endurance to be able to go through the trials. *"Strengthen my heart with endurance, so that I am faithful to you." "Give me patience and endurance in which Jesus walked. David and Jesus spoke of being consumed with zeal for God's house"* (Ps. 69:9; John 2:17). Another way to ask for endurance is by asking God to impart zeal to your heart. Zeal and endurance are two sides of one coin. It takes God's power touching our heart and mind to keep us from drawing back in our zeal and wholeheartedness. Ask the Lord to give you endurance or zeal to be faithful, especially in the difficult and dry seasons of life.

Love- Jesus is asked in Matthew 22 which is the greatest commandment in which He responds to LOVE the Lord your God and then proceeds to say to LOVE your neighbor as yourself. I think one of the main characteristics of Christ that sets Him apart is how He loves. He loves the least, the last and the lost, not just the well put together, the proper or whatever else but literally everyone. The interactions He has with all people show just how important love is in the life of a Christian. I went to a church in Toledo for some time and they would declare and pray this simple prayer "Toledo loves well." Ever since I heard that it always stuck with me and now I declare that over my life, family and continue declaring that over the city that I now currently live in. Love is super powerful and when believers fully love those around them atmospheres shift and chains break off. *Pour out your love in my heart by the Spirit so that I may overflow this love back to you and to others. In asking to abound in love, we are actually asking for the Spirit to inspire us in four ways— for greater understanding of God's love for us; for the Spirit to tenderize our hearts so that we abound in love for Jesus; to cause love for others to abound in our hearts; to love ourselves in the grace of God. Jesus commanded us, "Love your neighbor as yourself" (Matt. 22:39).*

Light of Glory- To make this super basic and easy to understand this one is referring to encountering the Lord supernaturally. Does God still speak today? Does God give dreams? Does God still perform Miracles and move in other supernatural ways? I personally believe the answer to these questions is yes. *"Let me see your light of glory and give me supernatural encounters."* Moses prayed to see God's glory, and afterward his face shone with the light of God's glory *(Ex. 33:18; 34:29).* We also can ask to encounter the realm of God's glory. Jesus spoke of an open heaven in which His disciples would see angels *(John 1:51).* Ask Him to shine the light of His countenance *(Psalm 4:6)* on your heart in such a way that you experience the supernatural realm of His glory, including receiving dreams and visions and seeing angels, etc. *(Acts 2:17).*

One Thing- Simplicity with this one. Seek the Lord. Keep the one thing the main thing. Engaging in our relationship with our Heavenly Father and seeking Him. *Remind me every day that I sit at your feet and build in me a desire to maintain a lifestyle of regular time with you. It is essential to spend time with the Lord—to be a person of "one thing" as King David was. David revealed his primary life focus when he prayed that the "one thing" he desired all the days of his life was to behold the beauty of the Lord, and to inquire in His temple (Psalm 27:4).*

Worthy- As Christians we need to believe that we are worthy to be His son/daughter. That comes with salvation and the understanding that we don't have to do it ourselves but we can trust in Him to be with us. We have to come to the place where we realize we can't go throughout our days without Him! He loves us so because of that fact we all are worthy to be His children and to step into the calling that He has for us. SO BELIEVE IT!!!! "But as many as received Him, to them He gave the right to become children of God, to those who believe in His name: who were born, not of blood, nor of the will of the flesh, nor of the will of man, but of God." (John 1:12-13) Due to our inheritance of being children of God we are worthy to receive blessings and all that He has promised us. *Strengthen my heart so I can walk in faith and obedience that is worthy of who you are and your calling in my life. Too many believers come up short of what God has invited them to walk in because of their half-hearted responses and choices. Jesus exhorted us to pray that we may be counted worthy to escape the snare of stumbling (Ephesians 4:1). Walking worthy of our calling includes being strengthened to escape the snare of compromise so that we stand in victory before God.*

Speech- This is one of those that doesn't need much explaining. I think Proverbs 18:21 sums it up pretty well, "Death and life *are* in the power of the tongue, And those who love it will eat its fruit." As Believers we need to watch what we are saying and how we say it. *Guard my lips and help me speak words that are pleasing to you, free me from impure speech. David purposed that he would not sin with his speech, so he asked the Lord to set a guard over his mouth (Psalm 17:3; 141:3).*

Humility- I think one of the most important things I've been learning these past few years is humility and the idea of going low. I never want to be someone who gets lost in pride. My wife went to a mission's school with Iris Global and one of the things she brings up when I talk with her about it is the consistent reminder the leader Heidi Baker would tell them of "going low and slow." Humbling ourselves before the Lord and letting Him use us for His glory and not our own. It's sad to see ministry leaders chase after numbers compared to chasing His glory.

In 1 Peter 5:6-7 it says, "Therefore humble yourselves under the mighty hand of God, that He may exalt you in due time, casting all your care upon Him, for He cares for you." Verse 6 makes it pretty clear in my mind…humble yourselves before God and He may exalt you in His time. It doesn't say to glorify yourself for saving certain people or healing certain people, the verse says humble yourself and give Him glory. *Teach me to set my heart to learn humility and walk in humility. Jesus called us to learn from Him about walking in humility or lowliness (Matt. 11:29)*

Insight- As Christians I feel we desire to know God more and more every day. That a primary part of being in relationship with Him is seeking Him and getting a deeper understanding of God. There are several scriptures that bring up the importance of seeking wisdom. Specifically James 1:5 and Proverbs 1:7 are ones that I wanted to share. James 1:5, "If any of you lacks wisdom, let him ask God, who gives generously to all without reproach, and it will be given him." And here is Proverbs 1:5, "The fear of the LORD is the beginning of knowledge; fools despise wisdom and instruction." In James it says those who lack wisdom ask God for it so that would include prayer. For the second verse it plainly says that you are foolish if you don't seek wisdom. With any decision, prophetic word, sermon you hear it is so important to go to the Lord with questions and seek Him to give insight and understanding of those things. Blindly trusting someone else's word without seeking wisdom from the Lord can lead you to some dangerous situations. *Give me insight into your Word, provide wisdom about walking intimately with you. The Spirit came to teach us all things—to give us insight or wisdom as He fills us with the knowledge of His will for each area of our life so we are able to walk in partnership with His heart (Col. 1:9-10). The Lord's desire is to give His people wisdom so that they are fruitful in every endeavor to obey Him and that they grow in or experience the knowledge of His heart in the process.*

Peace and joy- A theme throughout scripture is God's plan to bring peace, joy and hope. In the New Testament, Jesus brings joy to those who follow Him, and encourages others to do the same. The Apostle Paul also speaks of joy in his letters, urging believers to be joyful even in difficult circumstances. The Bible teaches us that joy is a gift from God, and that it is something to be celebrated and shared with others. For me the moment when I said yes to Him this indescribable peace and joy came over me and ever since then I continually want to live from that place of true peace and joy that can only be found in Christ. *Strengthen my heart with supernatural peace in areas that are troubling me. We do not have to live troubled by jealousy, rejection, anxiety, or fear, or with minds that are filled with turmoil, confusion, and indecision. If we regularly ask for peace and joy in specific areas of our lives, we will receive more of them.*

I pray that these tips will help jump start you into a deeper prayer life with the Lord. Hopefully I have done a good job of explaining and making them clear and easy to understand. I'm telling you these little tips help so much when you are stuck or in a rut. For the acronym even if you only go through a few of them the key is that it starts that conversation with the Lord. There have been some times where I've just straight gone through them all in a row but there have also been times where I might skip around. I might feel led to pray into the Fear of God and Insight and then the Lord might lead into something else but the key was just starting the conversation and getting it flowing.

Then the Holy Spirit might highlight one of the topics listed or go somewhere completely different. Before we go into the next topic I just want to bring back into our memory that we must remember WHO we are praying to and always keep that on our minds when we pray. I know I've said it a few times but if we don't believe who we are praying to then it's going to be hard to pray for miracles, healings, wisdom and etc. We need to stand on the truths of who God is everytime we pray!

| 4 |

Intercession

For some who haven't heard the word intercession before it may be an intimidating word. Most of the time if you hear this word you may think of older women who meet at your church and pray together or something like that. Literally as I'm writing this at Panera Bread there is a women's prayer group a few tables away from me. I mean in my case for a while I had that exact experience. I would go to a prayer meeting and I'd be with women who were double my age. The truth is that we are all called to be intercessors and prayer warriors. Like I shared in the beginning, I didn't understand prayer/intercession and the importance of prayer as a Christian until further into my spiritual journey. The word intercession itself means the action of intervening (stepping in) on behalf of someone else. Most of us probably do this in our prayer life without really knowing what it's called. If you are praying for someone else to get healed, receive breakthrough, or whatever it may be you are interceding on their behalf. Intercession is agreeing with what God will do.

The verse that I want to point out right away is from the book of Matthew.

Matthew 21:13

And He said to them, "It is written, 'My house shall be called a house of prayer, but you have made it a den of thieves.

Jesus speaks up after flipping the tables of the money changers and makes that statement. Jesus could have said many things after this but leans into the importance of prayer and specifically in the temple. He could have brought up many issues with what was going on in the temple but he focuses on prayer. In the Old Testament, God is speaking through the prophet Isaiah and makes a similar statement to what Jesus would later speak in the temple.

Isaiah 56:7

Even them I will bring to My holy mountain, And make them joyful in My house of prayer. Their burnt offerings and their sacrifices. Will be accepted on My altar; For My house shall be called a house of prayer for all nations.

God wanted His temple, His house to not only be a place where the Jewish people would worship Him but to be a house of prayer for all nations. He is calling His people to the place of prayer and intercession. The veil has been torn due to Jesus' death on the cross. We now have access to a relationship with our Father and don't have to go up to a mountain to hear God or give any sacrifices. We have His ear and can make our pleas to Him known wherever and whenever. It is in our DNA as Christians to be intercessors and to stand in the gap for those who can't. I firmly believe that in the days ahead prayer and intercession is going to be moving from a back room ministry to front and center. The church in the West stands at a critical juncture. The nations are increasing in lawlessness and moral confusion and engaging in escalating conflicts, including those inspired by racism, terrorism, and sexual immorality. They want to remove the influence of God's Word from society, because they see His ways as bonds and cords that enslave them (Ps. 2:3). David described Jesus responding to the crisis by praying, or *asking the Father*, for His rightful inheritance in the nations (Ps. 2:8).

One of the most encouraging truths that should strengthen us is to know that Jesus is forever making intercession on our behalf in the throne room.

Hebrews 25:7

Therefore He is also able to save to the uttermost those who come to God through Him, since He always lives to make intercession for them.

Apostle Paul considered this intercessory work of Jesus on our behalf important. In Romans 8 he pictured Jesus defending us against every charge or condemnation through His intercession. Isn't that amazing! Jesus is at the right hand of the Father right now! Again, we talked earlier about knowing who we are talking to and knowing that we have His ear as we pray and grow closer to Him. That fact should stir something within us to want to intercede and press in to see breakthrough, healing, restoration, etc. One of the things that bothers me and I know I can fall into it, is when we say "I'll be praying for you" and then not do it. I heard a lot of that when I first became a

Christian and didn't see people intercede and pray with me when I had a prayer request. It wasn't until I started going to a mid-week service when I saw people really get after it in the place of prayer and intercession and would contend week after week to see specifically the city of Toledo saved and for revival to break out. Seeing that impacted me and the Lord began to burden me to step into my calling as an intercessor and prayer warrior. Whenever someone needed prayer I was right there to be like "Hey, lets get after it!". That desire to see people set free and for cities to be transformed by the Gospel went to new levels when I began serving at a house of prayer. I had developed a history and relationship with the Lord where I saw transformation, healing, breakthrough, and atmospheres changing due to constant intersession and communion with Him. What if we really did pray for that person who is asking for prayer every time and don't just use that phrase to kind of push it off? Speaking to myself on that one too. With the world quickly becoming darker and darker we have to begin to wage war in the spirit realm and intercede to see His kingdom come, to see His kingdom on earth as it is in Heaven! A little freebie for those who have questions about Heaven, Randy Alcorn has a book called *Heaven* that gives the best Biblically based evidence I've ever read for questions you may have about what Heaven will be like. I say all of this to reiterate that it is in our DNA as Christians to be prayer warriors to be intercessors! There are countless stories about praying mothers, praying grandmothers, etc that have seen loved ones return to the Lord or know Him for the first time. We have to be a people of prayer/intercession! Who is going to pray for the lost? Who is going to pray for our nation? Who is going to pray for our schools? Who is going to pray for your city?

With talking about intercession I wanted to touch on being burdened for what burdens Him. Like why do we pray for Israel? Why do we pray for the ending of abortion? Why do we pray for the lost and things like that?

Romans 8:16-18

"The Spirit Himself bears witness with our spirit that we are children of God, and if children, then heirs—heirs of God and joint heirs with Christ, if indeed we suffer with Him, that we may also be glorified together. For I consider that the sufferings of this present time are not worthy to be compared with the glory which shall be revealed in us."

Paul talks of the joy that it is to suffer with Christ and share the burdens that He carries. Isn't that wild! From a worldly perspective there usually isn't joy in suffering. Paul recounts the blessing and joy it is to share that with Christ. So the things that He is burdened by we must be burdened by as well. For example a theme in scripture is God's love for Israel (Isaiah 43:1, Psalm 122:6, Deuteronomy 7:6). If you are not Jewish then you are a Gentile and this concept of the importance of Israel may be different and confusing to you. I believe that as the Church we don't talk enough about the importance of Israel in our faith. With the constant wars and attacks on Israel we as the Church need to continue to stand with Israel and pray for them. The Bible clearly tells of the importance of Israel and covenants He has made with the Jewish people. Just an example of how important it is to read the Bible and not just rely on someone else's word or opinion. In Genesis 12 it says, *"I will bless those who bless you, And I will curse him who curses you; And in you all the families of the earth shall be blessed."* This verse is one that I feel is important in recognizing our role to play for Israel. Not only does He say it will benefit us to bless them but it will also benefit Israel.

That is just one example that we can look to for knowing what burdens God. As you go through scripture you'll come across things that you'll recognize as something that He feels strongly about. As we read and get gripped by these things it will be easier to step into our role as an intercessor and it won't be hard to press in and spend time with Him praying and standing in the gap for this burden. Each of us might be called to intercede for something different due to our different lives and how we've lived and had different experiences. I'm a physical education teacher and I help coach baseball so I'm constantly around the youth, so it is easy for me to press in for them since I'm passionate about that age group. My wife on the other hand is passionate about human trafficking. It is a lot easier for her to be able to intercede for women who are trying to get out of trafficking and for trafficking rings to be eradicated. I'm not saying I won't pray into that topic because I have on several occasions but it might be easier to go after topics that we are passionate about. We all should pray/intercede for the burdens that are on God's heart. Constantly I'm asking God to burden me for what burdens Him, I want to see children filled with hope and joy, families restored, babies being born, racism smashed, the lost saved and more. Give us a deeper burning to pray for something that burdens Him. At the church I attend we have a mid-week worship and intercession night and lately we have felt led to pray for the seven mountains of society (business, education, media, religion, family, arts and government). I was leading prayer one of the nights and I can specifically remember praying for God to burden me with one of the seven that I really wasn't that passionate about. Right away business began to come to my mind. I'm not really a business-minded person, but it is so important to have Christ like businesses. For example, Chick-fil-a, is something that if we want to see transformation in our nation and beyond is so needed! Since that night, business has been on my mind in terms of entrepreneurship for myself and praying for those businesses who aren't afraid to proclaim Christ to be prosperous. I can remember a coffee shop (how Christian ha) that I would frequently gravitate toward who received backlash for not opening on Sundays and supporting a pro-life organization. We need to be praying for those businesses and praying for more of them to be established.

I really do believe that as believers we have to intercede for the seven mountains. There was a great document that I found from Loren Cunningham, founder of Youth With A Mission, that discusses the importance of each of the seven mountains in great detail. If you look at some of the major moves of God at least one or more of the mountains is affected by Him moving. There is a great documentary called *Transformation* by George Otis Jr. on Youtube that gives three examples where a move of God started by the Church praying for these seven mountains and a great revival broke out in these cities. If you ever have an hour of free time I highly suggest you watch it! It will stir you up to go after it in your own city!

Even right now as you are reading this, take a moment and begin to ask God to burden you for what burdens Him, or even ask what does burden you Lord? Open your ears and sit with Him if you need to and let Him speak. Maybe there is a passion you have that is burning in your heart, press into that! Let's say it's seeing the sick healed, start going after healing! Read and learn about healing and begin to intercede for the sick! Whatever it is and whatever the Lord burdens you with, let that lead you into intercession and develop deeper compassion in that area.

The more we experience the Lord and become burdened for what burdens Him I feel that it's a natural response that we would want to see other people encounter Him. At least for me that's how I feel, when I started experiencing seeing people get healed or having radical encounters with Him I just wanted others to get impacted by Him. I just wanted to see God move mightily wherever I was. At the time I was in a community who frequently shared revival stories and prayed for revival. This gripped me and hearing these stories stirred something within me to begin interceding for revival. I know that it is something that isn't always talked about in churches and communities. For the first year or two that I was saved I never heard of that term or that God could move in ways like that. I just feel that we need to be praying for revival and a move of God. I mean I've stated it a few times already but the world is getting darker, there's an identity crisis going on in our youth and the war for our souls is increasing. Shouldn't we cry out and ask God to move in radical ways to see people get delivered, healed, restored, and just impacted by the Gospel?

I taught a class on revival at the church I attend and for the first session we discussed revival stories. So we talked about Azusa Street, Hebrides, Jesus People Movement, Layman's, Welsh revival's and so on. After we talked about the stories I asked the people in my class, what similarities they saw in these stories? It didn't take long for the answer prayer and intercession to come forth. There's a great quote from John Kilpatrick, former pastor of Brownsville Assembly of God which experienced the Brownsville Revival from 1995-2000, that I feel summarizes the connection between prayer and revival perfectly, "Revival is birthed and sustained in prayer." I recently heard someone say revival won't come if we just continue waiting for it, we need to partner with the Lord and take action to see Him move because the time is now. To quote one of my favorite worship songs, Take Courage, "Simple obedience, it changes history." Those praying mothers from the Jesus People Movement wanted to see history change, they wanted to see their prodigal sons and daughters return to the Lord from getting stuck in the free love, psychedelic counter cultural movement that was taking place in the 60s and 70s. There is a fantastic book called *The Jesus People Movement* by Richard Bustraan in which he breaks down the movement statistically and a majority of the people who were saved in the movement had a previous religious experience and truly were prodigal sons and daughters. What if those parents didn't pray? I want to give a few more examples of the correlation between prayer/ intercession and revival if you are not as familiar with the stories.

The Layman's Prayer Revival or Businessman's Revival started with a simple prayer meeting at noon in a church in New York City, through consistency and hunger the meeting kept expanding by double everyday to the point where it overflowed into numerous churches around the city! Crime rates dropped during a time of rampant homicide and criminal activities, it's said over one million people were saved in a city of 30 million.

In the Hebrides Revival there were two sisters Peggy and Christine Smith who felt burdened to pray for the lack of youth in the church. Both crippled and blind in their 80s they kept praying. Peggy had a vision of young people filling the church, she contacted a Reverend in the area to organize a prayer meeting. These meetings began and months later a speaker, Duncan Campbell, came to preach which led to an outpouring of the Holy Spirit. A mark of this movement was the restoration of families and a return of young people to the church. The best thing in my opinion about this revival is that it is marked by very little backsliding.

There are a lot more revivals I could cover but lastly I wanted to talk about the Welsh Revival. In the beginning a group of young men began to meet and pray for the nation. One of these men was Evan Roberts. He started having encounters at night with God for two straight weeks that led him to intense times of travail and revelation. During a meeting after that two week period the spirit of intercession was moving on the congregation in great power. Evan was bursting to pray; then he felt the spirit of God prompting him to do so publicly. With tears streaming down his face Evan just began to cry: "BEND ME! BEND ME! BEND ME! BEND US." Then the Holy Spirit came upon him with a mighty baptism that filled Evan's heart that there would be no other theme of the great revival he would soon help lead. Evan began traveling around Wales and spontaneous prayer meetings began to spring up in schools, coal mines, factories and shops. During the revival, taverns were either closed or turned into meeting halls. Reports of hundreds of thousands were saved during this time.

There has always been a prayer movement that preceded a move of God. If we want to see God move shouldn't we begin to pray and intercede for it? I've probably said it a bunch of times already but if we truly want to see lives touched and cities transformed we have to stand in the gap and pray!

Being an intercessor is a part of who we are as believers and we have to step into that role everyday! Who is going to be praying for your family? Who is going to be praying for your children? Your spouse? Your friends? The list goes on and on, we must be a people of prayer and intercession!

| 5 |

Praying in the Spirit

There are a lot of different opinions on this topic that unfortunately have come to the point of dividing congregations and the church body. To start, notice I didn't title this chapter praying in tongues, which I do believe in and is a very important part of praying (just because you may not, I still believe you are saved) but I also think that since we are filled with Him through the Holy Spirit, when we pray according to His will we are praying in the Spirit. Praying in the Spirit literally is translated in the Greek to "with the help of" or "in connection to" the Holy Spirit. If our heart is in alignment with Him then I believe that we are praying in the Spirit since our hearts and minds are one with God.

Ephesians 6:18

Praying always with all prayer and supplication in the Spirit, being watchful to this end with all perseverance and supplication for all the saints

Romans 8:26-27

Likewise the Spirit also helps in our weaknesses. For we do not know what we should pray for as we ought, but the Spirit Himself makes intercession for us with groanings which cannot be uttered. Now He who searches the hearts knows what the mind of the Spirit is, because He makes intercession for the saints according to the will of God.

Praying according to the will of God not only assures us that He hears our prayers, but also that He will answer them in His own way in His own time. The key again is making sure we are in alignment with Him. As someone who's faith journey mostly has been in Pentecostal/charismatic atmosphere's I never really heard that the idea of praying in the Spirit most likely means praying according to His will. It really has helped me redirect any wrong thoughts or adjust my heart posture during my prayer time.

Since tongues are a topic that has a lot of different opinions and thoughts I wanted to focus the rest of the chapter on that.

1 Corinthians 14:18

I thank my God I speak with tongues more than you all

I mean Paul wouldn't have said this if there wasn't something important about tongues. It's also important to note the next verse where he mentions he'd rather five words of understanding to the Church than 10,000 in a tongue. Which I would agree with, again tongues is a Heavenly language and is between you and God. If there is a tongue for the Church then there must be an interpretation of that tongue. If there isn't then it would be a wiser decision to just speak in our native language.

Paul seems to have a great belief that there is something that is powerful and important about tongues or it wouldn't make sense why he would make such a bold statement. There are plenty of benefits of speaking in tongues. To name a few it connects us to the Father, strengthens us, speaking of mysteries, the enemy hates it, brings us into alignment with Heaven and it edifies God. I wanted to touch on a few of those that I believe are important.

When we speak in tongues in a devotional way, we commune with the Spirit who gives information that helps us to understand God's will and heart for us. Speaking mysteries is not about receiving "special truths" that are available to only a few. Paul was not referring to secret, elite information some might gain about spiritual things as the Gnostics claimed to have.

1 Corinthians 14:2

For he who speaks in a tongue does not speak to men but to God, for no one understands him; however, in the spirit he speaks mysteries

As our spirit communes with the Spirit of God, we may receive faint and subtle impressions from the Lord in the way that words of knowledge come to us. These impressions may give us insight as to how God wants to touch us or someone else through our prayers. They may be insights about our calling, life, or areas of brokenness and pain where our heart needs healing. Or the Spirit may show us something in our lives, such as the need to humble ourselves to someone or reach out in a relationship. Often the mysteries that the Spirit highlights are practical issues in which He wants to minister to us or through us. Paul spoke of the Spirit as searching the depths of God to reveal them to us. He is our glorious escort into the deep things of God's heart, Word, and will (1 Cor. 2:10-12). The Spirit possesses full knowledge of the Father and Son—one preacher spoke of Him as the ultimate "search engine" of God's heart. He gives us a portion of what He searches out as we engage more with Him by speaking to Him with our minds and by praying with our spirit.

Edifying oneself means being strengthened, or built up. Paul was encouraging them to "charge their spiritual batteries." Praying in the Spirit results in our hearts becoming more sensitive to the things of the Spirit (Jude 20). We may not feel anything when we pray in the Spirit, but we should not seek to measure what is happening by what we feel in that moment.

1 Corinthians 14:4

He who speaks in a tongue edifies himself, but he who prophesies edifies the church.

Jude 20

But you, beloved, building yourselves up on your most holy faith, praying in the Holy Spirit,

We bless and thank God when we pray or sing in tongues. Paul wrote that he who speaks in a tongue speaks to God (1 Cor. 14:2). Speaking in tongues is a gift that we use to bless, praise, and worship God in a way that differs from giving thanks only with our minds. Because we speak to God when we pray in tongues, we should specifically direct our attention to Him and not just speak mindlessly into the air. When I pray in tongues, I often focus my mind on the scene centered on God's throne in heaven (Revelation 4) and speak directly to the Father.

Whenever I talk about tongues I share this story a lot because it gave me a personal encounter of seeing the enemy get upset with hearing tongues. I think that is one of the better benefits of speaking in tongues. The enemy can't change your words around, he doesn't know what's being said and it frightens him.

I was in college and a friend of ours recently had given their life to Jesus. It was awesome she was on fire for the Lord and wanted everyone to know about Him. There had been a few nights where we worshiped and something would go on with her. One day I was talking with another friend about this girl and they had told me that they were just with her and saw something that seemed demonic. I'm talking, eyes roll back, blood in her eyes and trying to scrape out her heart. Some wild stuff that I've never seen in person before. My roommates and I happen to get a call that night about this girl having a manifestation outside of a dorm. We ran over and began praying and praying for hours. Unfortunately, that night there wasn't a breakthrough with things. The next night I get a call about something going on with this girl and if my friend could bring her over to our house. Our friend sits on the couch with a pale and dazed look on her face. We again start praying and praying and praying. At one point one of my roommates starts praying in tongues. Immediately as he does, I'm not kidding legit straight out of *The Exorcist* her eyes become more aware and turns toward him and in this creepy voice starts telling him to stop saying that and speaking that way. It was insane. Luckily, after hours of prayer the entity came out and she seemed to have woken from a dream and asked how she got to our house. Ever since that moment I refuse to watch horror movies (in general) with demonic or anything like that attached to it. To this day I still remember the power and confusion that was brought forth from my friend beginning to pray in tongues over her. If praying that way moved something in the Spirit I have to believe that there is something powerful and important about praying in tongues.

Speaking of tongues Paul described two different types of the gift of tongues, and two expressions with two different purposes. This helps us to better understand two statements that seem contradictory, that "not all" have the gift of tongues (1 Cor. 12:30), yet "all" can receive it (1 Cor. 14:5, Mark 16:17).

1 Corinthians 12:7-8, 30

But the manifestation of the Spirit is given to each one for the profit of all: for to one is given the word of wisdom through the Spirit, to another the word of knowledge through the same Spirit, Do all have gifts of healings?

1 Corinthians 14:2-5

For he who speaks in a tongue does not speak to men but to God, for no one understands him; however, in the spirit he speaks mysteries. But he who prophesies speaks edification and exhortation and comfort to men. He who speaks in a tongue edifies himself, but he who prophesies edifies the church. I wish you all spoke with tongues, but even more that you prophesied; for he who prophesies is greater than he who speaks with tongues, unless indeed he interprets, that the church may receive edification

In 1 Corinthians 12:30, Paul asked a rhetorical question, signifying that not every believer has the gift of tongues to profit the corporate body: "Do all speak with tongues?" In 1 Corinthians 12, the gift of tongues that Paul referred to was "for the profit of all," yet he wrote in 1 Corinthians 14 about tongues that bring personal edification to the one speaking in tongues. There is a difference between the gift of tongues given *to a few* for the *profit of the corporate body* (1 Cor. 12:7) when the speaker *speaks to men,* and the gift of tongues given *to all* as a devotional prayer language for the *profit of the individual* who speaks *privately to God* (1 Cor. 14:2, 4). Paul indicated that *all* can have the gift of tongues for their personal lives (1 Cor. 14:5, 39). Jesus included speaking in tongues as one of the signs that would follow those who believe (Mark. 16:17). Since tongues can be confusing at times, it's important to know the difference between the two types of tongues that are mentioned in scripture. Hopefully those brief explanations can give a better understanding of the two.

It is significant that Jesus mentioned praying in tongues in the context of the Great Commission. I believe we will be more effective in ministry if we include both casting out devils and speaking in tongues. They go hand in hand in successfully engaging in the Great Commission.

Mark 16:15-17

And He said to them, "Go into all the world and preach the gospel to every creature. He who believes and is baptized will be saved; but he who does not believe will be condemned. And these signs will follow those who believe: In My name they will cast out demons; they will speak with new tongues

Being edified in our spiritual lives by praying in tongues is an essential aspect of walking in the Spirit and ministering in His power. Often those who operate in the prophetic or the healing ministry speak in tongues regularly in their private prayer time. Like I have mentioned earlier, praying in tongues is a universal benefit for all believers. It is not a requirement or proof of salvation; rather, it is a benefit available to us through the work of Jesus and the indwelling of the Spirit. I'm sorry if you have been in a situation where a Church body has had that belief and made you feel "less saved" or something like that because of it. It is not reserved for those with a special calling. It does not require any special training, qualification, or preparation. It is a free gift to all as a part of the benefits of our salvation.

As I was first learning about tongues I had a friend tell me that I could ask the Lord for the gift, so I began asking Him for the ability to speak in tongues. A week or so went by with nothing, I then went to a mid-week service and that week a guest speaker from Africa was visiting. The service wasn't anything crazy or anything until the end. He had everyone come forward, hold hands and pray.

So that went on for a bit and he said, "someone who has never spoken in tongues before is going to tonight." I instantly was like…wow Lord I've been asking you about this pretty consistently over the last few weeks maybe it will happen tonight! After a while in prayer I was like well nothing has happened yet maybe it won't happen tonight and that's cool. Then all of a sudden a moment that has stirred within me ever since happened. The man was still praying, no one was touching me or anything, then this tingly sensation started to hit me from my fingertips and toes and made its way throughout my body right to my heart. I got weak in the knees and fell down, luckily someone next to me saw me going down and caught me before I knocked myself out. After a minute of laying on the ground this sensation came up out of me to begin speaking and I started saying things that I had no idea what was coming out of my mouth! It was a wild encounter that I can only believe was God. I know of people who have prayed and asked for this gift and it's taken time not as quickly as my encounter did but don't be discouraged! Continue to just ask the Lord to release this particular aspect of His grace to you. Some say, if the Spirit wants them to speak in tongues, then He will make them. However, the Spirit will not "force" any-one to speak in tongues. Some wait for an overwhelming sense of the Spirit, but often the Spirit touches His people like a gentle breeze. Therefore, as you pray for the release of the gift of tongues, you may simply feel the presence of God lightly or just a gentle urge to speak out. I encourage you to speak out the words that come to you and see what the Holy Spirit does.

| **6** |

21 Day Prayer Guide

I pray that this prayer guide would be a helpful resource to dedicate time and begin to flex that prayer muscle to where it becomes so natural to be with Him. Where you are getting lost with Jesus and stepping into new revelation and amazement with the King of Kings and Lord of Lords!

When praying about what to add to this guide these topics were ones that were placed on my heart to add. I've added scriptures that you can meditate on and prayer-read. You can spend as much time on each topic as you want, 1 minute or 30 minutes just come and be present for that time you are spending with Him! Let these just be a launching pad to deeper conversations and deeper intimacy with the Father!

Day 1

First Love

1 John 4:19 & Revelations 2:4-5

19 We love because he first loved us.

4 But I have this against you, that you have abandoned the love you had at first. Remember therefore from where you have fallen; repent, and do the works you did at first. If not, I will come to you and remove your lampstand from its place, unless you repent.

Day 2

Wisdom & Understanding

Epeshians 1:17

That the God of our Lord Jesus Christ, the Father of glory, may give to you the spirit of wisdom and revelation in the knowledge of Him

Day 3

Walk in a Way Worthy

Ephesians 4:1-6

I, therefore, the prisoner of the Lord, beseech you to walk worthy of the calling with which you were called, with all lowliness and gentleness, with longsuffering, bearing with one another in love, endeavoring to keep the unity of the Spirit in the bond of peace. There is one body and one Spirit, just as you were called in one hope of your calling; one Lord, one faith, one baptism; one God and Father of all, who is above all, and through all, and in you all

Day 4

Hunger

Matthew 5:6

Blessed are those who hunger and thirst for righteous-

ness, For they shall be filled.

Day 5

Burden Me for What Burdens You

Romans 8:16-18

The Spirit Himself bears witness with our spirit that we

are children of God, and if children, then heirs—heirs of

God and joint heirs with Christ, if indeed we suffer with

Him, that we may also be glorified together.

Day 6

Soften My Heart

Ezekiel 11:19

Then I will give them one heart, and I will put a new

spirit within them, and take the stony heart out of their

flesh, and give them a heart of flesh

Day 7

Apostolic Prayer

Acts 4:29-30

Now, Lord, look on their threats, and grant to Your servants that with all boldness they may speak Your word, by stretching out Your hand to heal, and that signs and wonders may be done through the name of Your holy Servant Jesus.

Day 8

Revival

Psalm 85 6-8

Will You not revive us again, That Your people may rejoice in You? Show us Your mercy, Lord, And grant us Your salvation.I will hear what God the Lord will speak, For He will speak peace To His people and to His saints; But let them not turn back to folly.

Day 9

Deeper Revelation of Christ

Colossians 1 10-12

That you may walk worthy of the Lord, fully pleasing Him, being fruitful in every good work and increasing in the knowledge of God; strengthened with all might, according to His glorious power, for all patience and long-suffering with joy; giving thanks to the Father who has qualified us to be partakers of the inheritance of the saints in the light.

Day 10

Fresh Encounter

James 4:8-10

Draw near to God and He will draw near to you. Cleanse your hands, you sinners; and purify your hearts, you double-minded. Lament and mourn and weep! Let your laughter be turned to mourning and your joy to gloom. Humble yourselves in the sight of the Lord, and He will lift you up.

Day 11

Fear of the Lord

Proverbs 1:7

The fear of the LORD is the beginning of knowl-edge; fools despise wisdom and instruction.

Day 12

Israel

Psalm 122:6 & Isaiah 62:6-7

6 Pray for the peace of Jerusalem: "May they prosper who love you.

6-7 I have set watchmen on your walls, O Jerusalem; They shall [a]never hold their peace day or night. You who [b]make mention of the LORD, do not keep silent, And give Him no rest till He establishes And till He makes Jerusalem a praise in the earth.

Day 13

Made into the Image of Christ

2 Corinthians 3:18

And we all, with unveiled face, beholding the glory of the Lord, are being transformed into the same image from one degree of glory to another. For this comes from the Lord who is the Spirit.

Day 14

Apostalic Prayer

Colossians 1:9

For this reason we also, since the day we heard it, do not cease to pray for you, and to ask that you may be filled with the knowledge of His will in all wisdom and spiritual understanding

Day 15

Pray-Read Scripture that is on your heart

Day 16

Pray in the Spirit

Day 17

Promises of God

Philippians 4:19, 1 John 1:9, 1 Corinthians 10:13 and

Deuteronomy 28:1

19 And my God shall supply all your need according to

His riches in glory by Christ Jesus.

9 If we confess our sins, He is faithful and just to for-

give us our sins and to cleanse us from all unrighteous-

ness.

13 No temptation has overtaken you except as is com-

mon to man; but God is faithful, who will not allow you to

be tempted beyond what you are able, but with the temp-

tation will also make the way of escape, that you may be

able to bear it.

1 Now it shall come to pass, if you diligently obey the

voice of the Lord your God, to observe carefully all His

commandments which I command you today, that the

Lord your God will set you high above all nations of the earth.

Day 18

Blameless Before Him

Psalm 15

LORD, who may abide in Your tabernacle? Who may dwell in Your holy hill? He who walks blameless, And works righteousness, And speaks the truth in his heart; He who does not backbite with his tongue, Nor does evil to his neighbor, Nor does he take up a reproach against his friend; In whose eyes a vile person is despised, But he honors those who fear the LORD; He who swears to his own hurt and does not change; He who does not put out his money at usury, Nor does he take a bribe against the innocent. He who does these things shall never be moved.

Day 19

Experiencing His Power

2 Timothy 1:7

For God has not given us a spirit of fear, but of power

and of love and of a sound mind.

Day 20

His Word Would Dwell

John 8:31-32

Then Jesus said to those Jews who believed Him, "If

you abide in My word, you are My disciples indeed. And

you shall know the truth, and the truth shall make you

free."

Day 21

Apostalic Prayer

Matthew 6:9-13 The Lord's Prayer

Our Father in heaven, Hallowed be Your name. Your

kingdom come. Your will be done On earth as it is in

heaven. Give us this day our daily bread. And forgive us our debts, As we forgive our debtors. And do not lead us into temptation, But deliver us from the evil one. For Yours is the kingdom and the power and the glory forever.

Amen.

Matt Cooper is a loving husband and father of one (for now lol). He currently resides with his family in Erie, Pennsylvania. Matt and his wife help lead a prayer and worship service at their church in Erie. He also teaches classes at their church with a multitude of subjects covering prayer, revival, hunger and worship. Previously, Matt has spent time leading a men's recovery group through the ministry of Celebrate Recovery and serving as a prayer leader at the Kalamazoo House of Prayer. Matt is passionate about prayer and intercession, the establishment of Amos 9:11 with the rebuilding of David's tabernacle, seeing the youth encounter Jesus and the body of Christ being equipped to grow in their relationship with Him. Outside of church Matt works as a Physical Education teacher in the city of Erie. He enjoys going to the beach with his family, playing sports, paddle boarding, hammocking and eating ice cream.

BOOKINGS

For speaking inquirings please e-mail
Matthewcooperauthor@yahoo.com

QR CODE

One Thing Collective Prayer Album